THE SURVIVORS OF *CHAURASI*

Poems on 1984 Anti-Sikh Violence

Ishmeet Kaur Chaudhry
Foreword by Girija Sharma

Printed in India

IndiePress

ISBN: 978-93-6045-185-1

First Printing, 2025

IndiePress

A division of Nasadiya Technologies Private Ltd.

Koramangala, Bangalore

Karnataka-560029

http://indiepress.in/

Edited by Ridham Bassi

Typesetting by MAP Systems

Publishing Consultant: Rechal Fernandes

Book Cover Design by Malik

Foreword

For someone to write poems after having edited a book on the same subject may appear to be a simple task. However, it certainly is not so. Ishmeet Kaur Chaudhry's poems on the 1984 violence, that was unleashed with the tacit support of the state, forcefully capture the immense trauma it left behind, jolting the readers into a realization of how conveniently the unforgettable agony of a community is often forgotten and how insensitively the Establishment tramples over the sensitivity of a brutalised people.

Black November: Writings on the Sikh Massacres of 1984 and the Aftermath (2019), edited by Chaudhry, furnished heart-wrenching and first-hand accounts of the Sikh massacres that followed the assassination of the then Prime Minister Mrs. Indira Gandhi. Appearing nearly five years after the publication of *Black November*, the poems in the present volume, bear out how deep the scars of the persecuted can be. The ferocity and heartlessness with which mass violence was perpetrated on the naïve and unguarded people in November, 1984 will remain one of the darkest chapters in the recent history of India. The poems powerfully portray the mindless fury of the mobs and the unspeakable trauma of the victims, which haunt many of us to this day. What strikes one is the fact that some of these pieces may or may not be 'poetic' in the technical sense of the term, as they seem to emanate from experiences which deeply and irreversibly disturbed the senses' repose—experiences which created images of shock, disbelief and horror in the deep recesses of the victims' psyche—images that were to keep gnawing at them forever. Hence, the irregular rhythms are but a reflection of the deep anguish of the victims. Perhaps, anything written otherwise, in keeping with the rules of metre and rhythm could not have captured that profound agony.

A sense of deep irony marks the poems. The chilling spectres of death and life are juxtaposed and one wonders whether it is life, or death in life, that delineates the predicament of the widows of *Chaurasi*. In their torturous and dreary existence, hope for justice is ever illusive. The concluding lines of 'Rest in Peace' bear this out:

...decades
 and decades
 and more years of injustice
how do you rest in peace?
Alive or dead?

Another poem 'A Chapter of Indian History' is equally evocative of their suffering:

We are the living dead
Skeletons of our past
Our bodies remind each one of you
That we are a chapter of Indian History.

The anthology brings to the fore a significant dimension of political, social and cultural antipathy that follows all pogroms. The massacre and madness of 1984 was no exception. Becoming 'the objects of sympathy', the widows of *Chaurasi,* were doled out charity by their own people, while for the powers that be they emerged as potent vote-banks: "…never forgotten during elections." The poems unambiguously refer to the negative typecasting of a community, not altogether unfamiliar in today's world. One is shocked into an awareness of how stereotypical and dismissive portrayal of communities/minorities leads to their marginalisation and consequent alienation.

Underlying all the poems is an acute pain and hopelessness. However, there are poems that convey a sense of hope and resilience—howsoever faint it may be—in an otherwise bleak scenario:

No matter how many attacks and assaults
…the whale doesn't fail to show up

The anthology concludes on the note that hope and cheer do not remain forever absent even in the midst of horror and violence; that peace and harmony will eventually return to this land, defiled with the blood of the unsuspecting innocents. The words of the Guru, quoted in one of the poems, celebrate the power of that undying truth:

The truth should be visible
the truth should be known and recognised
for the truth is ultimate….

November 15, 2024 Girija Sharma

Introduction

I was brought up in a very peaceful town, the hills of Shimla. During summers we had many visitors, mostly our relatives, from the plains. Whenever a new family visited us, *Chaurasi* (1984 anti-Sikh massacres) and *Santali* (1947 partition violence and migration) were an essential part of the discussions. Either my mother or my father would ask the guests about their experience during *Chaurasi* or the guest would ask us about any incidence of violence in Shimla in *Chaurasi.* The guests would narrate stories of survival, and we, as children, would sit and listen to them silently. Then our parents would take turns and tell them how we were saved by our neighbours when the mob attacked the gurdwara just opposite our house. Invariably, *Santali* was mentioned in these talks as a lament that we all were uprooted during *Santali* and now in Independent India we were still not safe. Or people talked about how their shops were burnt and how they bounced back, or some of them would talk of their struggle or difficulties they were facing as an after-effect of looting during *Chaurasi.* Sometimes the guests reported of some family member who went missing and never returned. While there were so many stories, there was one thing in common, everyone was still in a state of awe as they narrated their experiences. Tears would never fail them, accompanied by long pauses of silence, deep breaths and sobs.

These were not pleasant talks, nor were they pleasant memories. They were such memories that left behind deep scars. As an academician, I have tried to read and work on different subjects. I also think of moving away from *Chaurasi* and work on more pleasant subjects but invariably, I keep returning to it. Something inside me doesn't let me move on. Maybe, I am carrying an unconscious traumatic memory of what I witnessed as a child. Maybe, I would have been scared of being attacked. But I don't remember speaking to anyone about my fears or anxieties about this as a child. Maybe, that anxiety is resurging now and pushing me to voice these concerns. Finally, I have reconciled and I know that no matter how many areas I work on, *Chaurasi* will always remain central for me. I will keep returning lifelong inquiry for me.

I'm writing this Introduction while in Amritsar. Tomorrow, we're going to talk about another book on *Chaurasi. The Kaurs of 1984* by Sanam Suthirath Wazir. In addition to providing a first-hand witness account, he had collected the accounts of other Chaurasi women, including survivors, victims, women involved in the Khalistani movements, and the wives of militants. Every time I read these stories; I'm overcome with feelings of both guilt and gratitude that we made it through *Chaurasi* while so many others in our community couldn't survive. The shame that comes from having let them down, from not being able to support the survivors, from our community failing them, is another. Amritsar has so many stories, every citizen who was in Amritsar has been a witness to the events that shaped *Chaurasi*.

The women and the girls of Amritsar had their own challenges, the boys and men their own. The Sikhs on the whole, in those times, were vulnerable and so were women, both Sikhs and non-Sikhs. How do we register these concerns, how do we speak, how do we archive them? And why should we do all this, what is the need? Will this promise us recovery, or will this help us heal? I don't know. All I have are questions? All I know is that despite several efforts at my end, I am unable to move away from *Chaurasi* and it keeps pulling me back. After every talk on *Chaurasi,* I need a couple of days to recover from it, I need a few days to compose myself and get back to life.

I was six years old during *Chaurasi,* after Indira Gandhi was assassinated, the Sikhs were spotted and attacked at many places across India, for sure Delhi, Kanpur and Bokharo were undoubtedly worst struck. A group of people stormed the Gurdwara in front of our home, threatening to harm us as well, but our brave neighbor, Mr. Ravinder Randev, well known as Randev Uncle, intervened and dispersed the crowd. We were secure. This was one of the rare situations when friends help you without bothering about their own safety. For them humanity comes first. They risk their lives for you. So did our unsung hero. Without Randev Uncle, who knows what may have become of us?

These poems have emerged over years in different time frames at different experiences. Some were written following interviews with widows of the Tilak Vihar Widows Colony, while others were written after reading specific reports or after conversations with guests who shared their experiences during *Chaurasi*. They document the experiences of certain minorities who fall prey to political manipulation and vote-rigging. They are given a new narrative that shapes their identity and has been upsetting and troubling them for years.

These poems explore the question of how minorities emote while also experimenting with the poetic form. Certain poems might not seem to fit the traditional definition of poetry—perfect meter, rhythm, measure, metaphorical usage, etc. As an example, prose poems are most suited for some experiences that have been classified as predominantly narrative or prosaic. The poems lead the reader to experience the Sikh ways of life, the teachings and symbols; and the importance of five K's. While some people consider Sikhs wearing five Ks as fanatics or sometimes a threat, the five k's are deeply symbolic, they are important for self-upliftment and are used for the welfare of others. The poems address different facets of *Chaurasi*, as they also discuss the events that led up to the attacks, which included those on the Golden Temple in June 1984 and the events that followed Mrs. Indira Gandhi's assassination in October and November of the same year. They further discuss the ongoing impact of these attacks that the survivors are still feeling forty years after. The poems also discuss the bearing of certain events that recur every year, like Diwali or Guru Arjan Dev ji's martyrdom days. Diwali was just about a week before Indira Gandhi's assassination and Golden Temple was attacked on the anniversary of Guru Arjan Dev ji's martyrdom. Some of the survivors of the Tilak Vihar Widows colony, who were interviewed stated that they had not celebrated Diwali since Chaurasi and that the festival brought up memories of their prior traumatic experiences. A couple of the poems are autobiographical since they are based on my own experiences; these include the mob attack our family survived in November 1984 and the questions people asked us then, as well as they ask us occasionally now.

From my heart! Ishmeet Kaur Chaudhry

I

Life of the Widows of *Chaurasi*

Young girls, some newly-wed
lost their husbands to the Carnage in Delhi.
Then young widows- now old;
they refuse to recall those four days
and fateful nights
when women were gang raped
maybe… not at all like animals…
but like monsters…
Or
is it that humans are the only species
worse than ghosts and even *rakshasaas?*

Those who were dead died once
but the widows of *Chaurasi* have died many a death—
whenever the thoughts of that night
reminded them
of the shrill shrieks piercing the ears
of the helpless tears
of the weight of men on them hurting their backs
of the foul smell of flesh
of the darkest never-ending night
of the disgrace of blatant brutality

—they wanted to die
but the vulnerable eyes of their little children
their swollen faces
timid bodies
nervous minds
and the want of an embrace of the only parent left behind
forced them to live on…
The children wondered where their fathers, or
their peers or uncles, or the boys playing cricket every evening
had disappeared.

Only their mothers were left behind
unable to attend to the fears
anxieties
angst
grief
suffering
depression
trauma
of their children
for the mothers were the single bread earners.

The widows of *Chaurasi*
became subjects of sympathy
mere objects of charity
for the leaders of their community
and the political leaders of the nation.

They were never forgotten during elections
free distribution of blankets
and petty money
subsidies promised time and again
but never delivered.

But the widows only expected justice;
their feet once young, now old
refused to get tired
of the trips to the courts….
They had lost all—
even their children to drug addiction
who turned petty criminals
but what they retained was
dignity
and hope—for justice.

This was and is the life of the widows of Chaurasi

II

Secrets of the Past

Diwali night brings with it secrets of the past

Candles and lamps mark the festival of lights;
their glare blinds me
reminds me of that dark night
forty-years back....

The celebrations were not yet over

That time crackers burnt our houses
burning our men too...
white powder, kerosene oil and inflamed tyres
replaced the crackers.

The sounds of crackers

accompanied by
the screams of mothers
trying to protect the honour
of their daughters...

necks garlanded with burning tyres

turbans disrespected
beards razed
hair cut
cigarettes forced into their mouths…

screaming for mercy

with folded hands
helpless faces
tearful eyes…
shocked and muted, they breathed their last.

Diwali night brings with it secrets of the past

The sounds of crackers and the night brings with it
the era(z)ed memories of thousands of bodies…
the crackers—reminders of bursting gas cylinders
of fuming houses and mounds of ashes lying everywhere.

The festival is not welcome this year…nor any year ever since

no lamps and candles to be lit
for nothing can light up
the darkened faces and
the broken hearts.

(*In 1984, Diwali was on 24*th* October, and Mrs. Gandhi was assassinated on 31*st* October. During interviews, many children, belonging to families who experienced *Chaurasi,* stated that they have never celebrated Diwali since 1984.)

III

Rest In Peace

When someone dies, they say
"Rest In Peace"
But if the brutal hands of politics
Burns your men and children
Rape your women
Rip naked your daughters
Kill you with burning tyres and white powder
Humiliate you
Mock at your identity
Make fun of your hair
Handcuff you with your kara
Tie the string of your *kachairah* to your neck
and hang you till death on the tree
burn your kanga along with your burning body
stab you with your own kirpan
blame you for the crimes you haven't committed
followed by decades
and decades
and decades
and more years of injustice
how do you Rest In Peace?
Alive or dead?

IV

The Dead and the Alive

Why was I not killed when Sardarji was?
A question that has haunted me for years
and will continue to haunt me till the fag end of this tiresome long life.

Sardarji had left home for work on that fateful
morning of *Chaurasi*
like any other day…
but it was not the same…

The news came '*Indira Gandhi has been assassinated*
by her Sikh bodyguards'
…and Sardarji never returned…
from work…

They brought a truck full of corpses;
I looked everywhere for him, frantically turning each scorched body, trying to identify the face.
My fingertips sank into the tender, meshy, burned skin.

I turned one body
the next…then another…
they thought I had frozen with shock.

But I know
I was only seeking a last glimpse
to be able to believe that he was gone…

I have waited for his return
for years now…
four decades…

Deep in my heart I still harbour a secret hope:
maybe he is alive
and would one day return
to give me
one final look
before I pass away.

Forty years down the line
My incredibly long life is a curse…
and he must have passed away quickly…or…

God only knows how!
Whether he was severely beaten, burned alive or
garlanded with a blazing tyre…

V

A Chapter of Indian History

We are the living dead
Skeletons of our past;
Our bodies remind each one of you
that we are a chapter of Indian History.

Born in this country
we owned it, protected it,
were proud of it
loved it, nurtured it.

Our field yielded gold
we were the soldiers and
the farmers
the proud Indians

Till on a fateful day
history wrote an ugly chapter
justified it strongly
a mother was killed

Instead, they kill
her own children
maybe we were the foster children but innocent;
we did not kill our mother.

They called us militants
terrorists and anti-national
They called us many names
and we became a stock of jokes for them.

Then years passed
we lost our children to drugs,
depression and fatigue
in our struggle for survival.

They gave us charity
We needed involvement.
They took pity on us
We needed empowerment.

They said they would be brothers to us
We said we needed justice.
They said they will help us forget the dark chapter
We said we needed apology.

The fatal history
is adding to the dark chapters
prolonged years of injustice
and indifference.

VI

What We Know

She says we were crushed like mosquitoes
Some say we were roasted like *seekh kebabs*
While others say we were burnt alive and taught a lesson

What we know is that our 2-year-old Sukhdev was crushed in the stampede
while the pilgrims tried to escape for the fear of military
amidst the sounds of gunfire

Sukhdev's mother is blind now, weeping all these years,
guilty of letting him leave her hand and run away.

What we know is that Jassi *Bhenji*[1] was strangled to death with her own dupatta
What we know is that *Daarji*[2] was shot in his head
Both had gone for thanksgiving to the Guru

Jassi Bhenji and Daarji's shoes must be there amongst the unclaimed shoes lying at Darbar Sahib[3] *still*

---

[1] Women are addresses as Bhenji in Panjabi; literally meaning Sister
[2] Father
[3] Golden Temple

What we know is that two bodyguards of the Prime Minister shot her multiple times
What we know is that we were sorry for the manner of her killing
What we know is that the 'big tree had fallen'

A Sardarni remembered that her husband was fasting, mourning for the Prime minister's death, when the mob attacked and killed him

What we know is that thousands and hundreds of innocent Sikhs were butchered to avenge her death
What we know is that they were poor Sikhs and had no hand in her killing
What we know is that many of their children were brutally beaten to death

We have many and many more photos of our men and the little children, who were killed,
in the Gurdwara in 'Widows Colony'

What we know is that many men burnt our houses with white powder…within seconds
What we know is that many of our men were garlanded with burning tyres
What we know is that many of our women were gang-raped multiple times.

But no one talks about these women, they jostle alone with their bodies and trauma;
no FIRs were ever lodged

What we know is that we haven't been heard
What we know is that we haven't been given justice
What we know is that no one has tears for us in their eyes

Rather they call us terrorists at the smallest trigger…
they just have that word, they use most conveniently, to mark us

We know we were crushed like mosquitoes and roasted like kebabs
We know we have paid the price of the sins we never committed
We know we were treated like snakes in holes which they came to crush.

We know we are the soldiers who made numerous sacrifices for this country and its people
We know we have never asked for rewards and accolades
We know our fathers are poor hardworking farmers

Or

one of those soldiers killed at the border

But for sure we know
We are not the terrorists…
We are not the terrorists…
You blame us to be…

VII

My Little Mind Could Not Reason Well: A Prose Poem

That winter night,
as we watched from the window
we heard the slogan:

"khoon ke badle khoon." *
"Kuchal dalo sanpoon ko." #

Tension was in the air
as we anticipated the coming of the mob
knowing they would arrive

Mother forbade us from going outside to play
grandfather, father, and brother stuck to television, watching the news;
nothing was telecast

Just that some mournful music was playing throughout on the TV

I had never had such a boring
a holiday without reason;
I was bored.

Oblivious
that the reason could not be understood
by my little six-year-old brain.

...But I knew we were in danger

Our Hindu neighbour assured, "You will be safe Sardarji, don't worry"
he said, "No one will be able to touch you, *Darji*"
"We are here, dare anyone come in!"

The day was silent like the dead
The night shadowed us
and there was the mob

We switched off the lights

We peeped through the window and saw that
a mob stoned the Gurudwara opposite our house
a historical Gurdwara made by Maharaja of Patiala in his estate *Nabha House*

I, a six-year-old girl,
always fearless,
yelled abuses at the stone throwers

when suddenly, my brother shut my mouth

with his trembling hands;
I was suffocated
gasping for breath

he pressed my mouth so tight
I thought he was choking me
and he would kill me

I forgot about all that was happening outside

and I boxed my brother on his face
kicked him and
pushed him backward

He imprisoned me in his arms.
holding me tightly,
not allowing me to move an inch.

Then I gave up and settled in his tight clutches

Still in his clutches, I lifted my head
and looked out of the window
He whispered in my ears "If you shout this mob may come
and hurt us...be quiet"

I realised that my brother was saving us
and not attempting to choke me to death;
surprised and scared I became a mute witness to the scene
outside.

Our Hindu neighbour shouted at the mob

Three more Hindu men from our building joined him
They asked the mob to return and
stoned them.

The mob was diverted.
The *Bhaiji* at Gurudwara was hurt.
His forehead was bleeding.

He was a gentle man

He had the most melodious voice.
He sang *kirtan* day and night.
Why did they beat him?

I wondered
I never understood
I could not understand

My little mind could not reason well.

Just because two men had killed Indira Gandhi and they were Sikhs and wore turbans?
that is why we had a holiday and
was that the reason father and mother didn't go for work?

…but why did they beat *Bhaiji* who always sang
Ram, Ram bol, Ram, Ram….
And all my friends, whether Hindu or Sikh, always sang with him?

My little mind could not reason well
My little mind could not reason well

*Blood for blood/ #Kill the snakes

VIII

The Sikh Grandparents

White starched turban
crisp as Lay's potato chips
decorated the head of Sardarji
whom we lovingly called Papaji

Grandmother placed a vessel on the earthen stove—
a Sunday ritual—
preparing starch boiling rice water or flour
dipping the turban in it and let it stay

Two people were needed to spread it
on a rope to dry it
Once dried I waited to
bring it down

The turban would stick to itself
I would tear it open
the crisp *kach kach* sound
and the playful pulling it apart has its own pleasure

Badi Mummy, my grandmother,
would inspect the starch to see if it was patchy or evenly distributed
then fold it and put it aside

The days of starched turbans are gone
so have starchy Sundays
Gone are Papaji
and *Badi* Mummy

Many turbans were
burnt mercilessly…
not while starching them
but in *Chaurasi*

What remains is the memory
of the Sunday ritual
and the crisp *kach kach* sound
in some corner of our hearts

IX

They and We

They ask us:

"Why do you wear turbans?
Why don't you cut your hair?
You look like Rakshas…
and our women will never marry you
because you are hairy."

We tell them:

"We are natural. We live the way God made us.
The way our Guru instructed us.
The same Guru, who saved your women
when they were in trouble,
and that Guru's Sikhs protected you
when Aurangzeb was converting you forcibly.

"Guru Gobind Singh told us
to live naturally just the way God made us and
not to cut our hair
He asked us to stand for truth and righteousness.
That doesn't happen by hiding…"

They ask us:

'But why the turban?"

We shared our history with them:

"Guru Teghbahadar, Guru Gobind Singh's father
-a saint-soldier-
lion-hearted on the battleground
but utterly calm and composed otherwise.

'He was meditative, spiritual by nature
Though a warrior fighting for the rights of the helpless-
and the one who stood for justice
and never bent for sycophancy

'He sacrificed his life
for the rights of the Kashmiri Pandits
who were forced to convert
to Islam

'He propelled the right
of human beings to choose their faith
and have the freedom to practice it.
He was beheaded at Chandni Chowk in the national capital.

'The same capital where thousands of Sikhs during Chaurasi
were massacred, killed and garlanded with burning tyres
where innocents were butchered brutally
when everyone forgot or refused to remember our history/ their history.

'The storm accompanied the martyrdom of the Guru
there was zero visibility
when Lakhi Shah Vanjara, his follower,
stole his body, placed it in his house, burnt the house and cremated the body.

'Rakab Ganj Gurdwara, near the Parliament house today
is where his house was.
The same place where a memorial of Chaurasi has been made
housing photos of many Sikhs, little children who were slaughtered.

'While Bhai Jaita ji stole the head of Guru Teghbahadar
and took it to his son Guru Gobind Singh at Anandpur Sahib,
hiding it in a hay cart.
Guru Gobind Singh was nine years old then.

"On seeing the father's head,
Guru Gobind Singh announced that
a Sikh will always stand for righteousness and truth
and will have an appearance where s/he can't hide even if they steal."

The Guru explained:

'The truth should be visible
the truth should be known and recognised
for the truth is ultimate
The truth should stand out to
remind people of equality and freedom,

of humanity and justice,
of service to humankind,
of welfare and
well-being of all.

"The Sikh is a saint-soldier
Calm and meditative
But a mighty warrior
when there is a need to fight for the truth.
The turban adds responsibility
to stand out in the crowd,
to be recognised as one in lakhs."

They continue to ask us:

"That was the need of the hour, then. Why now?"

We tell them:

"The hour is forever...then, here and now
as the truth is for all times...
How can the dimensions of truth change?
Whenever evil forces rise
to curb the rights of innocents and
exploit them
the Sikh in the turban stands for the truth
as the truth never changes."

X

The Monster

The man in the turban
walked with pride
head held high
but with a humble heart
and high spiritual principles
addressed as *Sardar ji*
a man of honour
lively and joyful
always in *Chardikala*!

Dare anyone smoke around him.
People told their daughters to approach *Sardar ji*
in case they felt insecure on lonely roads
or trust the man in the turban while visiting strange cities.
They also defended the country
fighting battles on difficult borders.
They fed the hungry through *langar*
practicing the teachings of Baba Nanak.
Always in *Chardikala*!

How come the man in the turban became a terrorist?
Since when did the smokers intentionally blow the smoke of the cigarettes in his face?
When did *'Sardar ji'* change to *'oye Sardar'?*
How did the nation forget his sacrifices on the borders?
Why did no one remember the many times when *Sardar ji* filled their stomachs with *langar?*
But *Sardar ji* faced hardships
Brutal attacks
Betrayal and ingratitude
Moved on…always in *Chardikala*!

Communalism:
the monster led
hatred entered the hearts of people
this monster had sharp teeth and nails
that ripped apart *Sardarji's* hair and his head
this monster had robust hands
trained at throwing the incendiary white powder
this monster could hold
the burning tyres
and pull apart the limbs of
anyone who had the slightest resemblance to a *Sardar*

The monstrous politics of hate and the cheap vote-bank gimmicks swallowed the honourable image of the 'Sardarji' and turned him into 'Oye Sardar'

But *Sardar ji* accepted the will of God
and remained in ever-exalted Spirits
always in *Chardikala*
feeding *langar* to the hungry
fighting for the nation at the borders
yielding crops in the lush green fields
always in *Chardikala!*

XI

The Whale

The sheen of five and a half centuries
is losing its lustre
to the ways of the modern world
misrepresented histories
muted voices
stark silences
hidden faces
era(z)ing the traditions of minorities
to the culture of the majority;
the minority being sucked up in the waves of the ocean
but the whale doesn't fail to show up
...a reminder of its power and strength
of its existence and significance
of its prevalence and ubiquity

No matter how many attacks and assaults
...the whale doesn't fail to show up

XII

Motivation

As we talk of our woes
our elders share stories of our Gurus
their worthwhile lives
Sacrifices
Challenges
Resistances
Movements…
We rise
ready to face all challenges
head towards Karkardooma courts
or Patiala House courts
where piles and piles of our affidavits—tales of *Chaurasi*—lie
we hope for justice … in *Chardikala* … maybe someday
Our dead won't return though…

XIII

Strangers in Our Own Land

They regard us as weird beings
when we walk out in our vibrant turbans and long beards.

They gaze at our turbans and scorn our hair
showing their ignorance about their own history

They suspect our *kirpan* and doubt us for the *kara* we wear
as if we are out there to kill and not defend

They reject us like we are outsiders
because they don't like the way we look

We were born here and have always protected this land
regardless of the impact it has had on our families and our band

We had families where the first-born son was a Sikh
but now they find us as outlanders

Now that their identities have separated them from their blood
the brother is at his brother's throat

and

We are now strangers in our own land
We are now strangers in our own land!

XIV

Through the Eyes of a Child of Chaurasi

Too early in your life
you witnessed
the forbidden truth
of human brutality…
watching your father
being burnt alive
in the playground outside your house

your eyes will always
speak of the pain
you safely secure
in your heart
your body,
in your blood and veins
and inside you…

There is no letting go…there cannot be

XV

Scare

The bus stops in the middle of nowhere
The conductor shouts "Won't go any further, get down here"
'…Jeeto must be hungry' thinks Harbhajan Kaur
She walks to the next bus stop 3 kms away
it is turning dark from dusk
a scary winter night
the passengers from the bus have scattered
she is walking alone…
a shadow follows her
she runs
doesn't dare to look back
she runs faster
feels that the shadow is also catching up
doesn't dare to look back
ah! A sight of a few men…
takes a breath
panting… approaches them
asks them how far the bus stop is.
Doesn't look back
feels the shadow has stopped
remembers Jeeto…
tears well up

walks to the bus stop…
no sign of a bus
remembers Jeeto…
sees a few people waiting for the bus…
here comes number 8
will take it and change it after two stops…
It is pitch dark
hasn't eaten a morsel since morning
but doesn't care
only thinks about Jeeto…
finally, she reaches home
her feet as hard as the wooden plank
with bleeding blisters
Jeeto sees her mother
rushes to hug her
both embrace and cry their heart out
the little girl says "Good you came I was very scared"

"If only Sardarji were alive we wouldn't have been scared"

XVI

A Wish

We wish to erase 1984 from the century itself
and the 90's too

years of looting,
killing,
violence,
threat,
terrorism,
AK-47s,
betrayal,
attacks,
fear,
loss,
family,
young boys being lifted and killed,
girls raped and ruined,
encounters,
insurgency,
blood and dead bodies everywhere
multiple migrations and
political asylums
TADA,
POTA,
UAPA,

and replace these years with

Families rejoicing and enjoying the winter sun
having *sarson da saag* and *makki di roti*
with the Sunday ritual of oiling their hair
and washing them
with visiting Gurdwaras and
praying for the welfare of all
with working on our fields
and yielding a healthy crop
with celebrations on *Lohri* and *Baisakhi*
Gidda and *Bhangra*, singing Gurbani and distributing *langar*
with children studying for exams
and also learning *Gurmukhi*
with mothers singing songs
while combing the hair of their girls
with girls dancing and swaying freely
walking to their colleges and universities
with colourful *phulkaris*
with boys dashing on their motorbikes
trying to charm the girls
with matching shirt and *pagri*.

We long to have a peaceful Panjab, joyful and cheerful!

Credits:

Poems 'A Chapter of Indian History' and 'Rest in Peace' appeared in *Black November: Writings on the Sikh Massacres of 1984 and the Aftermath.* Edited by Ishmeet Kaur Chaudhry (Speaking Tiger, 2019)

Poem 'Rest in Peace' was also translated by Prithviraj Taur in Marathi for an anthology *Strikosh: Indian Women's Poetry in the 21st Century* by Prithviraj Taur and Swati Damodare (2021) This was also republished in *Nishaan Nagaara* (2023)

Poem 'Secrets of the Past' was published in *Nishaan Nagaara* (Issue 1: 2024)

Afterword

When you write trauma you live it all over again; and bring it alive anew for those who have experienced it and been touched by it in some way. Ishmeet Kaur Chaudhry's poems on the 1984 anti-Sikh pogrom, which engulfed major parts of India, show that facing trauma and healing are ongoing processes: they can never, perhaps, be a closure. Maybe due to lack of political will; but also because some tragedies lie too deep for tears. And closures.

Ishmeet's intellectual engagement with *Chaurasi* is well-known (her anthology *Black November* has been recognized as a major contribution to the genre); but these poems which she has written over the years, reveal her deep personal bond with the emotional upheaval, which is there to stay - for her and for the entire community; and which connects with national and global traumas of the century in a thoughtful and painful manner.

These are poems which bring to the fore the brutality of the massacres in graphic detail, when the *Chaurasi* widows were gang-raped by monsters, the young girls feeling the weight of the bodies of huge men raping them, ('the weight of men on them hurting their backs/ ...the foul smell of flesh') and the burning alive of men using inflammable powder and by putting tyres around their necks and setting fire to them, to name a few of the methods used to destroy the Sikhs for their ostensible role in the murder of the then Prime Minister, Smt. Indira Gandhi.

However, the poems explore various nuances of this violence apart from the physical decimation of the Sikhs. The damage sought to be done to their dignity and self-hood is reflected regularly in the poems: the cutting of hair to protect young boys, the mockery of the Sikh identity by making fun of their long hair, their *kadas* and the question to which they are subject for wearing the symbols of their faith and how well she portrays how the mockery turns to butchery

Mock at your hair
handcuff you with your kara
tie the string of your kachairah to your neck
and hang you till death on the tree
burn your kanga along with your burning body
stab you with your own kirpan

The aim of the mockery, obviously is the 'othering' of the community; since it is then so easy to unleash the mayhem on the 'othered'.

Then, there are the psychological, unhealable scars that remain on individuals and the community. The widows of *chaurasi* have had to live with the scarring memories, a 'living death' kind of existence while also bringing up their children, with minimal help from government or other agencies. 'Why was I not killed when Sardarji was?' is the nagging questions that remains in their minds. What can be more harrowing than the act of searching for a loved one in 'a truck full of dead bodies/ … My fingertips sank into the tender, meshy, burned skin', and the life-long memory of this harrowing experience? Having herself been a witness to the violence as a six-year-old, though not in all its horrifying aspect, Ishmeet's self-observation as an adult *'My little mind could not reason well…'* is both bewilderment and irony.

The most important question which the poems ask is the crux of all violence against the innocent members of a community which is held responsible for an act of a group of people from that community. In this case, who really can you hold responsible for the well-planned killing of Mrs Gandhi by two members of the Sikh community, who were acting at the behest of a few groups? What kind of revenge was it, which found satiation in the murder of innocent men, who were equally hurt by the assassination, of young boys, and in the rape of innocent women? It is tragic that the assertion 'We are not terrorists/ We are not terrorists' has to be made time and again by the Sikh community, the community, which Ishmeet points out has largely borne the onus of guarding the borders of the nation with their lives. It is in this context that the poem on the ultimate sacrifice made by Guru Tegh Bahadar ji to protect the Kashmiri Pandits from the diktats of Aurangzeb becomes even more significant.

Ishmeet has been engaging with the many aspects of *Chaurasi* - the well-planned and painfully executed killings in the cruelest forms, the rapes, abductions, the body blow to the Sikhs as a community, the widows of *Chaurasi* – Ishmeet writes them all, and the angst that *Chaurasi* has left in its wake has never been resolved. It would be easy to say that she writes about the most vulnerable victims of the massacre; but come to think of it, who among those dead and the ones who lost their dearest ones, among those who lost their livelihoods, is not among the most vulnerable? Even those who were too young to understand the full impact of 'inherited' these stories in their families?

There is a whole body of work on the *Chaurasi* pogrom and its after effects in the form of novels, short stories, poems, documentary writing, apart from films which explore the causes and ramifications of the tragedy. Yet it is a topic which can never be exhausted and each writing about it documents experiences which may be similar to the earlier ones, but then are not quite the same. Ishmeet's slim volume of poetry is a reminder that we have lived in harrowing times and the recurrence of such violent episodes has been legitimized by power systems, not only in India but across the world.

Charanjeet Kaur

Bio-Notes

Author

Dr. Ishmeet Kaur Chaudhry (educationist, author and poet) teaches at the Department for English Studies at Central University of Gujarat, Gandhinagar. She was recognised as an Inspired Teacher for The President of India's In-residence Program at Rashtrapati Bhawan, New Delhi in June 2015. She has been an Associate Fellow at Indian Institute of Advanced Studies, Shimla (2016-2019). She has been largely interested in areas of literatures of margins, studies of violence, trauma, and women studies. She has also been actively engaged in Comparative Studies and Translations from Punjabi into English. Her recent work has been on violence studies engaging with discourses on the 1984 anti-Sikh carnage in Delhi. She was recently given an award for her outstanding dedication and invaluable contribution to social welfare especially, on Women's Day 2024 by Aryavart- The Life Saviours, an Ahmedabad based NGO,

She is an editor of *Black November: Writings on Anti-Sikh Massacres of 1984 and the Aftermath (2019);* Patrick *White: Critical Issues* (2014); co-editor of *Violence, Subversion and Recovery: Women Writers from the Sub-continent and Around* (2019, with Rachel

Bari); co-editor of *Seeking Nanak : Commemorating the 551st Birth Anniversary of Guru Nanak Devji* (2021, with Paramjeet Singh and Charanjeet Kaur) and the author of *Life Sketch and Teachings of Guru Teghbahadar Sahib* (2023, with Jaswant Singh) and *Texting the Scripture: Sri Guru Granth Sahib and the Visionary Poetics of Patrick White* (2016).

Her collection of poems is *Forbidden Button and Other Poems* (Signorina Publications, 2020) Her poems have been published in prestigious journals like *Muse India, Culture Cult,* and *South Asian Ensemble.* and prestigious anthologies like *Yearbook of Indian Poetry 2021* and *Amity Peace Poems* by Shahana Ahmed. Her poems have been translated in Marathi for the anthology of Indian Women Poetry by Prithviraj Taur and Swati Damodar: *Stri Kosh: Bharitya Istri Kavita.* Her poems are being translated into Gujarati and Catalan (Spain). Her poems in Panjabi were published in *Preet Larhi.* Her interview was also projected on On Prasaranga Kuv (University of Kuvempu) page.

Dr. Ishmeet Kaur Chaudhry also engages in conducting talks on women concerns, well-being and mindfulness. She firmly believes that in a world that is full of pressures, there is an innate energy within human beings that can be positively channelised into making this world a better place. She engages in discourses on various aspects of spirituality, learnings from Guru Granth Sahib, and real-life memoirs.

She has delivered lectures in various institutions and different countries like Taiwan, Singapore, Australia, America, Pakistan,

United Kingdom, and Spain. Most recently, she was invited as a Guest faculty at University of Barcelona, Spain where she also delivered the 2023 Doireann MacDermott Lecture in April 2023.

Prof. Girija Sharma

Girija Sharma is a former Professor of English, and former Dean of Studies, Himachal Pradesh University, Shimla.
Her translations have been published in two volumes of the Writer in Context Series entitled *Krishna Sobti: A Counter Archive and Joginder Paul: A Writerly Writer,* both published by Routledge. She also translated a volume entitled *Taj Bibiwritten* by Rajendra Ranjan Chaturvedi for the series *SanjhiSanskriti ke Nirmata* brought out in 2022 by the Centre for Cultural Resources and Training (CCRT). Her translations also appeared in *Joginder Paul: A Reader* published by Sahitya Academy in 2023.
Her book reviews have been published in many journals including *The Book Review, Confluence (London), Summerhill (IIAS), The Beacon, Muse India, Indian Journal of Australian Studies and AKDA (The Asian Journal of Literature, Culture, Performance).* She has co-edited threeacademic books out of which two were published by Oxford University Press *(Echoes Across Cultures, 2003& Ripples on the Sands of Time,* 2013) and one by Orient Blackswan*(Reflections from the East and West,* 2012). She was also the Editor of Himachal Pradesh University Newsletter *Himshikhar*, a quarterly publication from 2011 to 2016.

Dr. Charanjeet Kaur

Dr. Charanjeet Kaur is a retired academician (English Literature), compulsive reader and occasional writer. She has been the literary editor and Chief Editor of 'Muse India - the literary ejournal', and is associated with Sound & Picture ARchives for Research On Women (SPARROW). She is also informally associated with 'EduSikh'. Her two volumes of poetry are: 'Mirror Image and Other Poems' and 'The Songs from the Hills' and is the co-author of 'Seeking Nanak', with Paramjeet Singh and Ishmeet Kaur Chaudhry.